NEVER WHAT WE WANNA SAY

NEVER WHAT WE WANNA SAY

DUKE LOTT

Contents

Copyright vii
Preface ix
Acknowledgements xi

1 They/We 1
2 Whitest Black Man 3
3 Lost In My Land 7
4 Hate 11
5 Away From Home 13
6 Smile-Cry Paradox 17
7 Days Back To Sunday 21
8 Question Of Existence 25
9 The Divide -1 29
10 Heaven Or Hell 33
11 Fearful Dictator 39
12 Philosophy Of Life 41
13 Power Of One 45

14	Woke Up with Love	49
15	Lifelong Traveller	51
16	The Power of Change	53
17	Earth Is Flat	55
18	House Across The Street	57
19	Forgive Vs Forget	61
20	Beauty Of Death	63
21	A Year Of Love	65
22	The Enemy Within	69
23	Love Is Waiting	71
24	Screams Of Humanity	73
25	Mountain's Sorrow	75
26	Normality	77
27	The Divide-2	79

About The Authors   83
Thank You   85

Copyright

Never What We Wanna Say
Written by Mayank Gangwar and Duke Lott

Copyright @ 2024 by Mayank Gangwar and Duke Lott

All rights reserved. No part of this book may be reproduced, distributed, or transmitted in any form or by any means, including photocopying, recording, or other electronic or mechanical methods, without the prior written permission of the publisher, except in the case of brief quotations embodied in critical reviews and certain other non-commercial uses permitted by copyright law. For permission requests, write to the publisher at the email below.

Publisher:
Genius Words
Pilibhit, Uttar Pradesh, India (262001)
Email: contactgeniuswords@gmail.com

Cover Design by: Genius Words

First Edition: June 1st, 2024

This is a work of fiction. Names, characters, places, and incidents either are products of the authors' imaginations or are used fictitiously. Any resemblance to actual events, locales, or persons, living or dead, is entirely coincidental.

Preface

It is with much pleasure that you join us in welcoming you to "Never What We Wanna Say" a reputable book that we seek to transform the lives of people by providing them with understanding through poetries, essays and stories full of knowledge and value.

We think, one should not consider only what is being said in it but how it was created as well. We aimed at giving voice to all, fettering none based on community, country, religion, or even continent. Hoping it is informative to have sought to establish a theory of universal acceptance while demarcating values that embody the essence of being.

Stretching across these pages are what many can identify as realities of life's hurdles. Our aim is to open the vision, to look at the world as the unity and to make people brave and to make a step forward. This book is an invitation, an invitation to take up new possibilities and to take action in your life.

That is why we invite you to join our endeavor and take part in the creation of the future. Let them be words for our souls to hold on to, to march forward in support of all our truths, and for the sake of togetherness.

For gracious thankfulness and best wishes,
Duke Lott & Mayank Gangwar

Acknowledgements

To our families, friends, and mentors, we thank you for your support amid challenges we faced during this initiative. Thank you for standing by us in a tremendous way all through the duration of this project.

To friends, the love and support that you have given us throughout doesn't go unnoticed.

To our team, every effort you have made to create this book was greatly appreciated.

To our mentors, it is with a word of appreciation to acknowledge your immense support, guidance and the part you played in this entire exercise.

We must acknowledge our sense of thankfulness to the Almighty God for empowering us in both energy and ideas to make this project a reality.

Last but not least, for all those who supported us and the concept of Universal Brotherhood and Progress, the toil to render this book deserves your appreciation!

With deepest gratitude,

Duke & Mayank

1

They/We

As a man,
He sees the world crumble,
The green took control,
Blue skies turn dark and gloomy,
Families, homes, economies tumble,
Destroying what was once theirs.

Will they/we be fine?
Will they/we survive?
Burning souls to feed their/our system.

Are they/we an experiment?
Can they/we come back,
Once they/we are gone.

They/we will never return,
they/we destroyed their homes,

they/we destroyed their families,
Now they/we destroyed their existence.

2

Whitest Black Man

(Do You See My Face)

I was told by a fellow human, who happened to be Caucasian or white, "You're the whitest black man I've ever met!" It was a total surprise. I was at a loss for words. Truth be told, it wasn't the first time someone had made this statement or comment to me, but it had been a long time. I didn't know what to say to him. Was he giving me a compliment, or was it something else? Was this his way of accepting me? How could he see me this way? I was hell-bent on knowing what he meant; I wanted to ask him questions. Before inquiring about his feelings, I had to think for a little bit. Did he say this because I'm polite? I'm black! How could he see me as white? I thought, I'm sure he can see that I enjoy my life; all was good, but was this right? To him, was I invisible? Does he see my face? If not, it's a miracle!

As I was getting ready to ask him, his friend walked up to me and said, "What's up, Black Honky," while laughing. I was like, whoa, what's that all about, with a friendly laugh. Trying to understand my position or disposition, my first question came in the form of a joke, "Should I take off my mask, you wanna see my face?" He laughed. I said, seriously though, how can you call me the whitest black man? He replied, you act white, but you're black. I said, what's acting white? I'm comfortable around you, he said, touching my shoulder. Our conversation was friendly, cordial, and respectful. I needed his honesty to dig deeper into how we see each other. Our whole lives, we are taught to look at color. Is it possible to look past color? My heart and eyes say yes! Instead of taking their statements as racist, I choose to learn more about how humans really see each other.

Our interactions can truly be about how we feel around a particular group or person. He told me it took a huge amount of courage to tell me; all he wanted me to know was that, as a white man, he felt comfortable around me, a black man. What's your opinion? Was his statement insulting? Was it a badge of honor? How would you take it? It seems society equates politeness and kindness to being white. A social norm. I'm curious as to why humans question race, ethnicity, and identity. I seek knowledge and understanding.

People come from various backgrounds, most with limited experiences in dealing with different cultures and people. The question I had to ask myself was, "How do you determine what blackness is?" Is it culture, movies, videos, sports, profession, etc.? I'm proud to be black! I'm proud to be African American; that's who I am. Black is beautiful! White is beautiful! Brown is beautiful! We are all beautiful! Let's get past what determines a person's beauty. Love the skin you're in.

How did I take our conversation? I handled it with grace. I said, "Thank you, kind sir, for those words of expression. Please don't feel the need to validate my blackness or my whiteness; accept me as a human being. What we need from each other is to try and understand who we are, together. Don't limit your thinking by what you feel, brother. Open your mind! Believe! Humanity is exciting! Embrace all cultures!" How do I feel about being called "the whitest black man"? It was weird! Also, an honor. To have someone in my life who doesn't really understand what they're saying but is so real about it, to feel it, try to express it, and explain it. What an experience! What a testament for discussion.

Lost In My Land

I walk through the streets,
people pass by, in their beat,
a laugh echoes,
a child's cries,
yet loneliness fills my eyes.

The park is green,
with children's screams,
a couple holds hands,
but I stand,
lost in my land.

A phone rings,
no joy it brings,
an empty call,
against the silent wall.

Night falls,
the city calls,
lights flicker on,
but my hope is gone.

Stars gleam,
in a distant dream,
the world spins,
but I'm trapped within.

A clock ticks,
the same old tricks,
time moves on,
but I'm stuck till dawn.

A bird flies,
under the skies,
freedom in sight,
but I lose the fight.

A tear slips,
from trembling lips,
a silent plea,
for someone to see.

The moon glows,
a cold wind blows,
but in my heart,
the darkness grows.

Through the pain,
through the strain,
I hold on tight,
waiting for the light.

4

Hate

I Hate dying,
Every time it happens,
I start crying,
I Hate feeling sad,

Why is everyone so mad?

I Hate goodbyes,
It always makes me sigh,
Followed by
a question of why?

I Hate fights,
I have bad dreams at night,
I Hate Time,
Watching it unwind

And rewind,
I Hate pain,
I wish life wasn't so vain.

I Hate pictures,
Sometimes they're triggers,
I Hate violence,

Especially when humans remain silent,
Can we all just get along,
The same version,
The same song,
Hate,
Are you a feeling,
Or just a strong word?

Regardless,
You keep eyes blurred,
I Hate you, Hate,
I can't wait to see your fate,
Your face is blank,
Love will always win,
So I embrace you with
Thanks.

5

Away From Home

Mother's mental health has been slipping, and I'm worried! Her episodes are more vivid, and the scenes more intense and terrifying. Mother brought all of us kids this time. The diaper bag was full of diapers, bottles, and all the usual belongings that usually accompanied us when we were away from home. The strange thing was, this time Mother brought more blankets than we would usually take. It was weird that I noticed; it made me very suspicious and uncomfortable.

While in the car, I began to wonder and couldn't figure it out for the life of me. Lately, around the house, Mother hasn't been paying attention to us kids like she did in the past. She was always right on top of things. As the oldest, I would notice and help. Mother didn't really have to watch me. My sisters and brothers have been enjoying more freedom, running around the house like crazy, yelling, screaming, and fighting. When Mother did say something lately, she would completely lose her temper! Mom is a very soft-spoken lady, not much to say. Now, that's not who Mother is. Her temper is very strong and scary. Dad is never around. Always gone. When he is home, all he does is lay on the couch, eating and drinking his cheap whiskey.

Mom has been crying a lot lately, especially at night. The other night, I swear Mother was having a conversation with a man, but Dad wasn't home. I actually heard it with my own ears and saw it with my own eyes. I opened the door to see Mom all alone, talking to a man, but there was no man there. She was sweating, cursing profusely. I walked into the room and said, "Mother, who are you talking to?" She replied, "No one!" Then a glass flew off the table, loudly breaking on the floor, scaring the life out of me.

These conversations between Mom and the man, whom I now know she calls Crowley, became more frequent and violent. She tried to hide it, but it became apparent that Crowley was making Mother mad, sad, angry, and violent. The nasty cuss words she would use around us kids seemed so dubious that I began to seriously worry, as Mom never cursed. Mother was having another conversation with Crowley, and it seemed like they were arguing about Mother killing people. She was trying to refuse. It got interrupted by the kids, my younger siblings. This conversation with Crowley ended with Mother frantically crying. The next conversation between Mom and Crowley made me worry about the safety of us kids! Is Mom going to make us vanish? It seemed Crowley was telling Mother that she needed to get rid of us and Father.

6

Smile-Cry Paradox

Life examples for smiles and tears create rather paradoxical picture in the taffety of human life. The dining experience and the man versus self-conflict, which at their core seem so different, are in reality intertwined. Further considering of this paradox leads to the deep philosophical consideration of feelings, experience, and the very existence.

Being a sign of happiness one of the most basic facial expressions may hide something else and will be depicted in the story. It can be a smile, and behind it, there may be keen, suffering, grief, or perhaps hesitation. The lie of a smile may warm to the eye but a storm brew in the heart filled with peace and hatred. As for the second set of opposed values, tears are conventionally linked with sorrow and suffering; however, they can also symbolize liberation, purging, or sheer joy. Thus, crying as an action is not just associated with sadness, but it is a purging activity which enables the soul to be purified and the heart to be mended.

The smile-cry paradox is a perfect symbol of bipolarity of the human condition. This speaks to its theme, which seems to explore emotion's layers and perplexing nature, forcing people to question what they feel. A smile may mean that the patient is accepting the situation, strong, or the true feeling is happiness even if it contradicts most of the features that characterized the patient until the time of the accident. Likewise, tears could also mean a person's soft or weak side, compassion, or when a human bond is deeper than most. It can be said that both these feelings are real and true and that one cannot exist without the other because life, as is well-known, is a beautiful blend of happiness and suffering; joy and sorrow.

Detailed Comparison

1. Authenticity vs. Facade: Another type of smile is the fake smile; this smile does not come from within, as opposed to a natural smile, it is only a pretense. While the first one defines real and spontaneous emotions, the second one depicts fake and insincere crying or tears.

2. Expression of Emotions: Whereas smile, which is a cultural sign of happiness, love or laughter, tears are feelings of sad, empathy or relief or joy.

3. Catharsis and Healing: Crying serves as a cathartic release, allowing us to process and release pent-up emotions, leading to emotional clarity and healing. In contrast, a smile can uplift spirits and create positive energy, contributing to emotional well-being.

4. Social Dynamics: Smiles are often shared in social interactions to convey friendliness, warmth, and connection, fostering bonds and building relationships. Tears, when shared, can deepen emotional connections, evoke empathy, and strengthen interpersonal understanding.

Ultimately, the beauty of the smile-cry paradox lies in its capacity to evoke profound reflections on the human experience. It teaches us to embrace the complexity of emotions, acknowledging that joy and sorrow are intertwined facets of life. By embracing both smiles and tears, we gain a deeper understanding of ourselves, our relationships, and the intricate dance of emotions that define our existence.

7

Days Back To Sunday

Shining like the sun,
Sunday,
has the week just begun?

Resting the day before,
seems to be the one.

Sunday,
I long for your day to come.

Monday,
I stare at the moon,
light in the midst of darkness,
shining the brightest,
strawberries in June,
you make flowers bloom.

Tuesday,
I see your hand,
splitting waters from land,
today,
our Earth was made,
as I gaze,
walking in the shade,
I prayed,
for our planet on the way.

Wednesday,
Much more than midweek,
a hump day,
or day to play,
I see visions,
past and present,
desired the most,
before Friday,
the mercury,
I feel personally,
time to fish,
it's 80 degrees,
I'm leaving work early.

Thursday,
A blessed day,
you are,
a time to heal,
donating,
showcasing,

generosity is real,
to your abundance,
I bow and kneel,
I pray,
then meditate,
on your goodness,
lucky me,
the pureness,
the fullness,
whispering,
telling me to visit family,
I listen to you,
happily.

Friday,
I Love You,
I'm in love,
the start of the weekend,
our time should never end,
Friday,
you're my friend,
TGIF,
the day of Jesus' death,
so glad it wasn't his last breath,
just a test,
if you don't know the truth,
I suggest,
a request,

we're blessed,
don't stress.

Saturday,
A Day of rest!
Are you the first day,
or the last day,
many opinions,
truth I pursue,

what say you?
SUNDAY!

8

Question Of Existence

It's important to preserve our existence. To maintain the "we," the presence of the "I" is just as necessary. If you don't know who you are, you can't tell them who we are. To save civilizations, protect your own existence, and this isn't about advancing by harming someone else's existence. Challenging someone else's existence is foolish, just like pulling someone back to move forward yourself. It's wise to reject anything that creates division among us. Ultimately, remember that "I" is not greater than "we," but when "we" are wrong, "I" should face it rather than fade into darkness. Truth doesn't always win, but it must always fight against falsehood. Just like in war, where soldiers on both sides give their best knowing only one side will win, every effort to protect the truth is valuable. When you die, you won't be called a coward but a martyr.

We are more than merely a species fighting for its life; we are a civilization that holds a certain set of values, morality, and our own community. Basically, any society cannot subsist without the support of integral and developed personalities of the 'I' type. All the confusion results in the emergence of instability, division, and the end of civilizations.

In every respect, the existence of a person is valuable and should be honored. Everybody should have the right to be themselves and not have to constantly fear for their lives or be discriminated against for it. Self-worth is a strong predictor of individuals, and as a result, these people create an atmosphere of mutuality within society.

Thus, there can be found numerous examples in history when the problems of existence – oppression, suppression of rights, or denial of identity – called for revolutions and movements for change. One can think of civil rights campaigners, women who underwent intense struggle for their rights to be recognized and minority groups that did not accept any repression. Their fight was not only for themselves but for all the others and for the "we" so many people long for – for a world in which the lives of all are appreciated.

When the going gets tough, the tough get going, or it may feel like the world is closing in on one. One aspect of gaining true strength is accepting the odds or hurdles in front of us and fighting with vigor and zeal. We cannot allow divisive politics in our world; we are stronger together.

As is the method of soldiers defending their territory and principles, so must we be staunch on our ground of truth and justice. The way may be tough, but each taken step takes humanity to a realm where mere existence is not only safeguarded but is embraced.

Thus, it remains important to underline that 'I' is not more important than the 'we': it is the 'we' which should become stronger and more persistent in building the better future for everyone. When facing the difficulties that life presents and working on the development of the most important values, the basis should be: truth, integrity, and unity.
United We Stand!

9

The Divide -1

"They" proclaimed wars and "We" were sent to battlefields, losing our lives while "They" further fought for their distinctions.

While "They" put sanctions, he said, "We" would starve and get desperate, our children going to bed with their stomachs empty.

"They" held the power and the authority and enforced their uncalled-for laws and "We" had to live under oppression.

"They" and their luxury laughed while "We" and our suffering lived with silent weeping.

"They" promoted hostility and "We" suffered physical aggression; our groups dismantled.

"They" fostered envy while "We" fought for our self-esteem status diminished, our aspirations smothered.

"They," fumed and growled with hatred and "We", got slammed and our hearts and our bodies hurt.

"They" made us shiver, "We" were deemed helpless and our spirits were subdued to dust.

It is about time "They" wounded our souls, and "We" pain, Yes, our souls were never sutured.

Looking at the history "They" inflicted damages not only to the land but "We" also saw our homes collapsing, our roots destroyed.

"They" brought frailty, and "We" struggled to be mighty, our strength threatened.

"They" kept us illiterate and "We" craved knowledge, we were left in the dark.

"They" sowed poverty and "We" rot; groaned and moaned and cried and sighed and screamed and tore; if "We" tried not to waste our potential, how?

That was a racism "They" practiced and "We" the oppressed fought for our equal rights our native identity stripped off from us.

"They" said we are not as good as them, and "We" believed them, and thus the decline of our identity.

"They" established the world for "We" where we were wrong; guilty of sins that propelled from their bias setting.

"They" placed us into dinner sets of sin and Sleaze, convincing us that we are inherently sinful and the best depiction of evil.

As for "They," they continuously deprived us of opportunities, and as for "We," they closed the doors in front of us and trampled our dreams.

"They" were able to dictate whom our societies were and what our stories were, "We" being denied these histories and our stories.

"They" erased our truths, "We" cast aspersions on our realities, "We" were told we are insane.

"They" ensured that everyone was the same and "We" changed to fit this mold, individuality dead.

"They" collects our wages while "We" worked so hard; where is our worth?

10

Heaven Or Hell

Thinking it was the day of judgment, the Pastor fell to his knees to pray. Confessing his sins, he thought the rapture he preached about was happening, and he was left behind on Earth for the numerous sins he committed. All his fears were taken away when his assistant pastor, a God-fearing man, came into his office asking him, "Did you feel the earthquake?" "Yes sir," he replied, "I thought it was the rapture!" He said to himself, "I gotta get my life right."

At that moment, his cell phone started ringing, calls coming in back-to-back. His mother, wife, children, and family were all calling at the same time. He answered them all, putting one on hold to answer another, assuring everyone that he was safe and all right. Then another call came in; it was his mistress, Lindsay. A beautiful, tall, long-legged woman who was a member of his church, she was invited by another church member.

Reluctantly, he answered the phone as he walked into the other part of the church. He said, "Hi baby," she said, "Hi sweetheart," he replied, "Are you all right?" "Yes, I'm fine," she said. "How are you?" "I'm just thinking about you and the next time I can see you," he said. "I'm a little tied up right now. How about 4:30 pm before the 7:30 night service? I'll drive over to our usual spot, see you before church, and then after the night service, I'll come back for a nightcap, honey." "Ok," she answered, "Can't wait to see you and feel you." "Me too, baby," he said, as he hung up the phone, smiling as he walked back into his office, answering phone calls, FaceTime calls, praying for people, giving them advice on sin and life, and taking confessions. Not really thinking about any of that, but only about Lindsay's soft body, her blonde hair, blue eyes, and nice bottom that he loved.

Trying to focus and convince himself that it was time to get ready for Bible study, he sat down at his desk, put his phone on Do Not Disturb, and went to his notes to prepare. Two hours flew by, and it was 3:30 pm. The Pastor started to think about what was keeping him up at night, a nonexistent sex life with his wife Maria. 3:30 pm also meant it was time to go because the hotel where they met was about an hour away. They met 60 miles away, so that it would be far from town, limiting the chances of them being caught.

The plan was to make sure that they weren't being followed, and for Lindsay to take care of all the arrangements so that there was no paper trail that could connect to the Pastor. Not only for domestic home issues, but the affair was a pain to hide, the church funds, parishioners' tithes, and offerings. The money from the church was paying for the extracurricular activities and all of Lindsay's undergarments. He liked her to dress in sexy Victoria's Secret. He liked red!

As he jumped into his new Cadillac, his phone rang; it was his wife, Maria. He answered and said, "Hi honey!" She replied, "What are you doing?" He said, "Nothing, preparing to do God's work." "OK honey, I understand God comes first, but I wanted to ask you a question." "Shoot," he said. Maria answered, "I need you to answer me on why you haven't made love to me for almost 2 and a half months? When I try to touch you, you push me away or tell me you're tired or that you have to do something for the church. Is there something wrong with me?" "No honey," he said, "It's just the position I'm in, all that I have to do, what I'm responsible for. It sometimes gets to be very stressful, and everything gets to be too much sometimes, but I'll fix it, and I'll make time for you." "Ok honey, I understand," she replied, being a good pastor's wife. "Just be careful, please dear. You are in a position of power, the trials, and the numerous things that a woman may do for a man in your position. The power bestowed upon you is the ultimate turn-on. I was with you before you were the Pastor of a big church, and I was there when you didn't have two nickels to rub together. Don't mess this up; don't mess up a happy home." He replied, "I love you, baby, and I'll see you at church. Bye."

Speeding just a little to get to the hotel, his destination, the room already reserved, Lindsay waiting inside, he went in through the back way, which was always part of the plan. He walked up to room 231 instead of taking the elevator. When he arrived at the door, himself already ready, Lindsay opened the door in a see-through red lace bra, red stockings, and very thin red underwear with red bottom heels. Her body was silky with lotion that had small tints of candy apple red.

She spun around to reveal that she had a new tattoo on her bottom. It was a heart with PDH inside of it, which stood for Pastor D. Holmes. He said to himself, "I've got a problem here." His thoughts were quickly erased by Lindsay unzipping him with her mouth. She was just inside the door, on her knees with him standing in front of her. It turned him on so much that the moisture in the air he received was starting to bring him closer to climax. Not wanting that just yet, he pushed her gently to the floor, then picked her up and softly threw her on the bed, letting his animal instincts take over!

As the clock struck 6:00 pm, Pastor Holmes put on his clothes, bid Lindsay a fleeting kiss, and stealthily left the hotel room and headed back to the church. He entered the church just in the evening service an emotion of guilt and relief overwhelmed him. Stepping into the church he saw families heading for pews, children playing, and people praying.

That day the mood was tense, people were focused and filled with respect. Inhaling deeply to calm his nerves, and ensuring that his smile was as wide and genuine as possible, Pastor Holmes walked towards the lectern.

Just as he was about to begin the service, a little boy, approximately eight years old, ran up to him and grabbed the hem of his robe. "Pastor Holmes can i discuss something with u?" the boy asked hesitantly. The Pastor knelt down to the child's height so as to listen to him carefully and kindly. "Of course, my child. What do you want?" The boy looked at his friend with clear and sincere gaze when speaking. "My parents say I lied to them. So, am I going to hell now? Will God show me a path to heaven?"

11

Fearful Dictator

Dictators aren't afraid
of questions from journalists,
but of poets writing
about love.

They know revolts
begin not in papers
or movements,
but in poems.

They're scared
that soldiers with guns
might turn into keepers of love.

They're afraid
the youth in their rallies
might walk the path of peace.

They're scared
that those fighting over faith
might unite in love.

They fear poets;
they know one day,
they will be dethroned
by poems written on love.

12

Philosophy Of Life

The concept of pleasure and happiness imply a kind of cyclical character, which occurs when a person chases after that which he or she wants. The OPT provides direction to our activities and choice-making by revealing purpose, thus assisting in managing through difficulties and maintaining focus using resolve.

People should not avoid circumstances that make them feel nervous since this means they are going out of their comfort zone, which is very important in the end. This logic goes through the reasoning process of learning from experience; it also goes through the process of practicing more so as to gain mastery of life's events.

There is a way that we live our lives, the thoughts we harbor in our minds and how much we truly desire something determine how that something becomes a reality. From the analogy of the cycle of life one is able to grasp the concept of the transience of life and the need to embrace life fully regardless of the stage one is in.

Embracing transitions and doing something towards the things we want in life eliminates possible future regrets and cultivates satisfaction. Time is one of the most valuable commodities and a notable motivator to make relevant decisions and change for the better to grab available chances.

Accepting the raw bits of life also means accepting the rough, it's embracing chaos is to appreciate the beauty of genuine and tenacious. It is important to ensure that a good record is left behind by performing laudable deeds to continue impacting the society.

Laws for a Perfect Life:

1. Law of Pleasure and Satisfaction: Their passion often sees pleasure as an ideal to be attained only to leave one with nothing every time one achieves the ideal.

2. Clarity of Purpose (Why vs. How): This is done in order to know the right approach to take when pursuing the objectives, goals and aims in the organization.

3. Law of Least Effort and Comfort Zone: People tend to act according to the principles of reactance theory, choosing the easiest route, hence, to find solutions beyond comfort zones it requires an effort.

4. Learning through Practice: Education is a process of acquisition and therefore should not be overemphasized on planning unlike what others would like to make it appear to be.

5. Law of Attraction and Mindset: The totality of this judgment underlines the need to think positively as our thoughts attract that which we have focused on.

6. Cycle of Life: Our existence is characterized by developmental stages that go through curiosity of childhood to the experience of old age.

7. Acceptance and Action: Thus, learning to accept what is and to take action in the present will reduce future regrets and encourage the experience of satisfaction.

8. Seizing the Present: Concerning time, people always stress that time is money and should not be wasted; therefore, there should be no delay.

9. Embracing Impermanence: Some of the characteristics included in this tradition are the acknowledgement of the impermanency of life which in turn inspires people to live fully and embrace every moment.

10. Legacy and Impact: Making followers and the world a better place contributes to meaning in life after one's lifespan.

In the complex scheme of things these laws, these philosophies, these messages all fuse together to provide a guide to a life of perfection. If one is able to focus on the principles of clarity, resilience, authenticity and purpose then it is possible to live a life that is built, understood and led effectively with greatness and leave behind a legacy that will make a difference.

13

Power Of One

Comrades,

Today I introduce to you a force that never tires, a force that can only be harnessed, as it is termed, 'The Power of One.' All of you have the power to open doors, turn worlds around, and start fires that can burn down establishment.

On the legends that started from one single man, warrior, figure all on his own. Mahatma Gandhi an individual inspired a fire that burnt away the chains of subjugation. Rosa Parks, a black woman, stood up for the black race, against discrimination by refusing to give up her seat to a white man; thus, igniting a fire of black freedom across the world and the entire black continent. Joan of arc fights the armies and leads nations with ONE vision.

Open your eyes to the all-defining picture of mankind from the times when one bear and one cry broke the chains of vulgar indifference. Today we remember Martin Luther King Jr. and ONE dream he had that set the society on fire for justice. ONE Nelson Mandela resolved once tore down the walls of apartheid and call for unity. Alexander the Great, ONE man, dreamed a dream and subjugated kingdoms, joined continents.

They spoke strong not just as single persons, but as enlarged representations of the Power of One. Their stories are timeless, they tell us that it all starts somewhere, with a stride, a chant, a vision.

Oh, my brothers and sisters do not under rate the single force that lies within you. In your veins, flows the blood of determination, the strength of ethos, and the hope of endurance. You are not just ONE; you are a force to be reckoned with.

The Power of One deals with the ability of an individual to thrive in a society that is filled with problems. Let it course through your system like fire and let it be the driving force in you, on the pursuit of reform. You will be prepared to withstand any pressure and is ready to roar in the vastness of time and space.

Hear this, yes hear it clearly, you must love who you are because that's what transforms the world. Maximum effort should be aligned to your voice, for it is the battle hymn of constant advancement. Take the word 'Power' seriously in the phrase 'Power of One' for it is perhaps the root and foundation of success in you.

Rise, my comrades, rise! Let the One in you rise and create a world beyond boundaries and beyond the horizon for generations to come. The world is yours for the taking, its waiting for your spunky, your nerve and your passion.

Thus leaving no one behind, but hand in hand as ONE, let's rewrite the future, reinvent the future and etch it in the sands of time. For in reality, we are not just people, but activists fighting for the society's cause, fighters who believe in hope, creators of a new future.

Make the Power of One our cheer, our goal, and our victory!

14

Woke Up with Love

I woke up next to you. It wasn't a face or eyes I was staring into. It had nothing to do with outer beauty. So, writing this love letter is my duty!

It's a wonderful thing, you lying next to me as I sleep throughout the night. Indeed, I know you're there; I'm not worried or frightened. I feel joy as you hold onto me so tightly. You promised never to let go of me, promised never to hurt me! The warm feeling you give puts a smile on my face. Whispering in my ear that you'll always be with me, that it will be okay. No matter where I go, to be with me for eternity.

When heaven calls, you will follow me, staying with me until the end of time. Even through mistakes and bad times, never saying, "Goodbye." Can I take a picture? When I look, all I see is a photo of me! Are you there? Oh, I see you, Beautiful! With the smell of flowers, your taste is like a box of fine chocolates. Let's light some candles, have a nice breakfast. These roses are for you.

Thank you for sacrificing yourself for the benefit of our relationship. You're silent, that's why I listen to you. Our moments are magical, emotional because you listen to me. Never self-centered, focused on growth, remaining unchanged, "Love is Love." Pure in expression, unmatched in essence. Always there, no boundaries. Loving me first! Also taking the time to love others. No evolution needed.

Sometimes I sacrifice sleep for you. Why? Because you make me reach deep inside to find all I need and want. Love, you make me want to love more. I seek you more than riches. Your wisdom is what I truly desire; I surrender.

The light in a sometimes-dark world, your gifts, given daily, conquer all! Your love is a decision, always asking, "What Can I Do for You?" Your acceptance has helped me develop inner peace and contentment. Prioritizing you has helped me help others achieve their dreams and goals. I appreciate you; I'm keeping you in high regard. Self-love, you're not selfish. You're an act of kindness towards me!

15

Lifelong Traveller

Beyond all civilizations,
we search for-
our own histories!
Those eyes still wait
for their beloved to come.
The burden on the head
is eager to be lifted now.

Saying "just a little more,"
who knows how many journeys remain.
With endless desires in my heart,
I set on new journeys!

In adverse circumstances,
I recall
those who left behind

their essential belongings;
the words that
were never spoken,
gradually unfold
on the wrinkles of my forehead.

The hidden person in my poem
seeks
a remedy for their suffering!
Journeying is a must;
So is arriving
at our own abode
fatigued and worn!

But to claim
that all shall reach home
is a jest
for those without shelter
for those who venture
under the blazing sun
crossing human bounds-
they travel for life!

16

The Power of Change

The power of life and death is within the tongue. Written words confuse many. I want to be precise, my friend.

Don't just look in the mirror; look inside yourself. Do you like what you see? Never underestimate the power of change. Change is so powerful, but only if you do the work. You have to get up and drive yourself, make it happen. Do the things necessary to ensure that you are successful. You're going to have to lose sleep. You're going to have to give up things. You're going to be tired; keep pushing. It's going to be tough; keep working on becoming the best version of yourself. What do you want to be? Do you want to make the most of your talents? The question is yours to answer. Get up, stand up, make it happen. Love yourself first. You have to love yourself first; then you can love others. When you love yourself first, the possibilities become endless. The journey is the reward. Continue to evolve; it takes time. Be content. Work extremely hard, but work smart. Have a plan. Develop your plan, write it down, read it every day. Stop making excuses! Don't make assumptions; nothing is certain. You get what you give. If you haven't already, start now! The power is in the now. All you have to do is believe in yourself. The universe has a way of opening doors for those who try, believe, and have faith.

17

Earth Is Flat

Dear poet,
your poetry made someone believe
in their lover's return.
So those eyes waited forever
for their beloved to come back,
hoping that since the Earth is round,
they would meet again someday.

But when their beloved didn't return,
they outright denied
all science and facts.

They declared,
"The Earth isn't round; it's flat.
Those who leave don't come back."

It was said with such certainty
that there was no room for doubt,
for who would ever doubt
a poetry?

18

House Across The Street

I see you out of my window,
the trees fill my view,
a branch falls,
after giving it its all,
our world seems so small.

When I see you,
I say hi,
you never reply,
not even a goodbye.

Home,
Gone,
please leave the lights on,
regardless,
I know you're there,

no need to stare,
the sun glares,
the sky is blue,
fresh air,
flowers bloom,
a "No Parking Sign"
you have room,
a truck zooms,
to park in your spot,
making you very hot.

A red cardinal lands on your sunflower,
all happening in one hour.

Your balcony watches life,
the view is spectacular and speechless.

As the seasons change,
you get new paint,
a better, bigger gate,
why hide your estate,
Wait!
A listing date,
please don't sell,
Mademoiselle,
I'm calling you on my cell,
no matter the price,
I would buy you twice,
now you're mine,
So nice.

19

Forgive Vs Forget

Soft echoes of old words
greet the morning light.
The harsh tones are forgiven,
but the sting remains.

Children are playing
and laughing by the river.
Some losses endure,
such as misplaced games and toys.

I forgive the lie told by a lover
who broke a promise,
but trust is brittle.
Memories persist.

Dates missed and minor errors are forgiven,
but they persist.
They stay silent for a while.

I overlook imperfections,
but their sighs and anger cut deeply.
They remain in the silence.

We let go of minor aches and
forget minor injuries,
but some deeds remain.
I'm not angry with them,
but the hurt is still there.

20

Beauty Of Death

Me trembling on pages,
with an impractical attempt
to complete my poetry to the fullest.

Not all ends are happy endings,
and so does life,
yet the thought of glorifying death
wasn't my choice.

I didn't aim
to be an irresponsible poet
who left his art incomplete.

But all I could do
was write things
which were cringe to some,

romantic to others,
and a disaster to me!

Now, writing about life,
all I can think of is an abrupt end.
My pen is falling from my hand,
with watery eyes,
I bid farewell
to the poetry left behind.

Life's beautiful, but how will they know?
So is death, but how do I find it?
Time to check out both, goodbye Poet,
your desk needs rest...

21

A Year Of Love

Our love lasted like a year!
It began with chilly winds;
All emotions frozen like ice,
Desperately trying to break free.

Then you came –
Into my garden;
Like a hint of spring.

And suddenly, everything came alive,
Countless desires took over my heart.
I was filled with energy,
Singing songs of triumph.

Time passed,
Spring turned into scorching summer.

Enduring the heat,
We saved ourselves and travelled far away.

We waited eagerly on a sandy bank,
Our hands clasped together,
For the arrival of the monsoon.

And it finally came!
Like a figment of imagination,
In the drops of rain,
We saw it –
Love, revived under the scorching sun!

Certainly, it was beautiful,
Filled with boundless joy.
I would look at your beauty in amazement;
Lost as if in some wonder!

But who knows why?
Some cruel winds blew,
And my garden turned barren!
Yes, it was autumn,
In which I, like a tree,
Kept withering away.

When I reached it,
The plant I had cultivated,
Even its leaves had deserted it!

Indeed, it was autumn,
In which I, like a tree,
Kept withering away.

Now the chilly winds are blowing again.
Emotions are frozen within,

But this time, they're not trying to escape!
They're staying inside,
Bottled up and suppressed.

Because after this cold season,
Spring will never come.
No one will await anyone!
The garden has become desolate,
No more saplings can be planted!

This weather affects not only the garden,
But also the gardener –
The one who spent his entire life nurturing it!
The flowers will never bloom again...

22

The Enemy Within

The enemy walks near me.
A shadow in the blaze of the day,
Cold and constant.

A weight on my chest.
Somehow, we proceed through it,
Shoulders heavy with worry.
His whispers are like a chilly wind,
Feeding on my unease.

His eyes were dim but probing.
Throughout my hidden worries,
Which are fueling my doubt.

We push ourselves to stand steady,
But his hold contracts, choking us.
Every advance is a battle.

He creates impenetrable walls,
Mocks my efforts, and feeds off my sorrow.
But we're not alone.

In stillness, a flame burns,
Strength grows in our fists,
And rebellion fills each breath.
We rise from the shadows with a last push,
Our will annihilating the enemy's shape.

Now that the sun has come up,
It is evident to us that
We have defeated our fear,
Which was the enemy.

23

Love Is Waiting

In love, are mere union, separation, and pain enough? Are these words truly all there is? Beyond them, within their very essence, lies a universe where anticipation and dedication reside. There are those who are in love or within love, and there are those who transcend it. Yet, there are also those who may not be in love but are waiting—waiting for an eternity. Those who cannot attain the union of love become immersed in dedication, and when suddenly someone arrives one day, we realize that we lack the means to hold onto them.

Love constructs, and destruct too—construction is of energy, and destruction of self, because love doesn't permit harming others. Love is not bondage but liberation from bonds.

No one has the right to define the meanings of love; everyone has their own interpretations, but it's essential that once a definition is established, it must be fulfilled. Just as my definition of love is unique, "Love once, and love hard." Just as every philosopher wants to reach their ideology to the masses, I too want to etch my definition in people's memories. Yes, I'm not a great philosopher, but an extraordinary poet, an author, and much more that is still seeking within me. I am extraordinary because love is never ordinary.

What is love, how is it, how much, when, why? Who knows, because answers to questions change from person to person. For some, it's like a flowing sweet lake with a lot of noise, while others see it as burning embers in winter. What's really true and what's false, who knows, who needs to know? And even if you find out, will the meanings of love change, will the ways change? No. Love remains the same, and you will find it where you belong despite circling the earth millions of times. Lovers keep moving in endless journeys, but love sits there waiting.

This article will meet you in the end, so that after traveling the entire world when you return, you find love waiting!

24

Screams Of Humanity

The echo is loud,
walking through the halls of death,
cold,
in the air,
I see breath,
holding on by a thread,
ugliness continues,
sick,
wait,
the menu,
my order,
time is getting shorter.

Sir,
please stop hitting me,
what are you doing,

I ain't going nowhere,
get out of here,
you were evicted days ago,
a violation of us all,
shall we walk or crawl,
no longer ignoring destinies' call,
I feel sorry for you,
Ha, Ha, Ha,
don't leave,
stop playing,
we can do more,
stop,
no you do not,
you poor soul,
why be so violent,
shut up,
silence,
no rights here,
no more can you live here,
I thought we were cool,
we're family,
none of this to you is here,
don't fear,
a new day will appear.

25

Mountain's Sorrow

"Letting go was love, maybe that's why I couldn't stop you..." In our lives, we encounter so many moments when, despite our desires, we can't stop the person who matters the most. With a heavy heart, we say goodbye, and sometimes, we don't even get the chance to say it. It's undeniably sad to part ways, but even sadder are the moments after, each breath feeling like a heavy stone passing through us.

We can't stop everyone, but we can try to let someone know that they matter to us, and ask them to stay with us, together...

When we look back at the passing moments towards the horizon, the empty sky gazes upon a rugged mountain. Those I couldn't meet often appear in my poems. I've never been able to bear someone parting from me. When I go to the mountains, loneliness can't touch me. Whenever I call out, I hear you. The mountains walk with me, and at the summit, we share our sorrows. The mountain's sorrow is greater than mine, but it never gives up. It finds joy in bringing happiness to others. Watching tourists come and go, it wants to belong to them, struggling hard to hold itself back. It knows if we don't meet again, its life will pass in waiting. But still, it loves immensely. Eventually, when we return, it waits there for us. Look – right there, the mountain is waiting!

26

Normality

\

I see a woman,
treated as if she isn't the mother of the earth,
responsible for birth,
invaluable,
is her worth.

Is it normal to disrespect a woman?

This deserves a different reaction,
no matter how hard,
a few,
groups of people,
in power,
try to keep it the same,

Normality,
needs a change.

An illusion created by society,
fit in,
be nobody,
fear being out of place,
it's okay to hate,
balance,
equivalent weights,
sensitive or thick-skinned,
let's translate,
the usual happenings of everyday life.

What is normal?

Life's personal experiences are unique,
watch this video,
is how we speak,
turn a blind eye to the casualties,
Normality or reality,
brutality, mortality,
what about vitality,
no desire to restore you,
what most people do.

27

The Divide-2

"They" reduced our mobility, and "We" were always confined and denied our liberty.

While "They" were provided with all they needed, "We" were stripped of all our basic necessities.

It is them who defined how much we are worth, and it is us who agreed and crumbled with their words.

"They" shoved their thoughts down our throats, and "We" challenged the essence that we hold dear: faith and spirituality.

"They" prescribed what we should do or be, and "We" complied with what "They" wanted us to do, leaving our capabilities unused.

"They" watched us, in turn, "We" were the closest thing to prisoners in what was essentially a virtual war against our rights.

It was "They" speaking their language, while "We" were forced to write in a language that was not ours and was barely tolerable.

"They" convinced us that "We" are the issue; they instilled their bias in our minds.

"They" set up the system of social injustice, which is the mechanism that entrapped and restricted our progress and existence.

"They" deprived us of our basic rights, our freedoms, and our humanity, making us mere pawns in their grand scheme.

"We" felt the weight of their oppression in every aspect of our lives, from the food we ate to the air we breathed.

"We" bore the brunt of their greed, their fear, and their hatred, our existence a testament to their cruelty.

But in our suffering, we found strength; in our pain, we found resilience.

"They" may have defined our past, but "We" will define our future.

"They" may have tried to break us, but "We" will rise from the ashes, stronger and unbroken.

For every act of oppression, there is a spark of resistance; for every injustice, there is a call for justice.

And as long as "We" remember our worth, as long as "We" fight for our rights, "They" can never truly win.

In the end, "They" will be remembered for their cruelty, but "We" will be remembered for our courage.

In the annals of history, "They" will be the oppressors, but "We" will be the survivors, the warriors, the ones who dared to dream of a better world.

And in our dreams, "We" will find the strength to break free from their chains, to build a future where "They" no longer hold power over us, where "We" are truly free.

About The Authors

Duke Lott

Duke Lott, Host of "The Duke Lott Show," is a Certified Crisis Prevention Instructor, Motivational Speaker and Diversity Lifestyle Coach based in Michigan. He is also a 2024 Rosalie Petrouske Poetry Award Recipient. As a former collegiate tennis player, Duke learned how to communicate with people of all different races, creeds and colors, which he uses to inspire changes in how people view, deal with and discuss race relations. Upcoming projects include a children's book and his personal memoir, "Fear Led Me to Faith".

As a motivational speaker, Duke Lott is an inspirational personality that has worked in the Inner City for over a decade. Serving as Program Director for non-profits, Duke discovered his passion for Mentoring and Public Speaking. A former Radio Board Operator for Country Music and NASCAR. Duke is an Author/writer. His books include: 100 Lessons For A Successful Interracial Relationship and Fear Led Me To Faith, coming soon.

Reach out to Duke here: linktr.ee/thedukelott

Mayank Gangwar

He is the visionary founder of Genius Words and holds the position of Executive Producer and Lead Host on the "Dear Paarijaat" Podcast Show based in India. Mayank is a prominent figure in the field of book publishing, podcasting, and music production. He continues to make significant contributions as a multi-talented creative and entrepreneur on the global stage.

Internationally recognized as a book publisher, song producer, author, poet, podcaster, lyricist, debater, and social entrepreneur, Mayank wears many hats on the global stage. He is the author of the book 'Artistic Yogi: Journey of a Changemaker,' the editor of 'The Gentlemen' by Mthobisi Magagula, and the translator of the Hindi version of the international bestseller '100 Lessons of Interracial Relationship' by Duke Lott, co-author of "Professor Sahab" and "Talk with the Moon." His musical collaborations include producing masterpiece songs like, 'Kinaara', 'Tera Saath' and 'Angaar,' with Prakhar Chitravanshi, and 'Artistic Yogi' with Granth.

Reach out to Mayank here:
linktr.ee/mayankgangwar

Thank You

To all those who read and felt inspired,

Thank you for being a part of this journey. Each page of this book is a testament to the power of words and the potential for change. We invite you to bring that change, to be the change. It only takes ONE step forward to make a difference!

We have done our piece of contribution, and now it's your turn. Spread the love, spread the word! Let's stand together against discrimination and oppression. It may not change today, but ONE day, with our collective efforts, we can make a difference. So put in your efforts, share this book, and gift value to others. Maybe, someone out there needs it more than you know!

"Never What We Wanna Say" is the voice of all, a voice of Universal Acceptance. Together, we are ONE.

Blessings to you all!

Duke Lott & Mayank Gangwar

www.ingramcontent.com/pod-product-compliance
Lightning Source LLC
LaVergne TN
LVHW051956060526
838201LV00059B/3681